AFRICAN TEXTILES

CHRISTOPHER SPRING

CRESCENT BOOKS
NEW YORK

ACKNOWLEDGEMENTS
THE AUTHOR WOULD PARTICULARLY LIKE TO ACKNOWLEDGE
THE HELP AND ADVICE GIVEN BY JOHN MACK AND HELEN WOLFE
OF THE MUSEUM OF MANKIND, LONDON AND BY JOHN PICTON
OF THE SCHOOL OF AFRICAN AND ORIENTAL STUDIES, LONDON.
HE WOULD ALSO LIKE TO THANK HIS WIFE YVONNE FOR HER PATIENCE AND
SUPPORT THROUGHOUT.

DEDICATION:
FOR YVONNE.

PUBLISHED BY CRESCENT BOOKS
DISTRIBUTED BY CROWN PUBLISHERS INC.
225 PARK AVENUE SOUTH
NEW YORK, NEW YORK 10003

AFRICAN TEXTILES
REPRODUCES A SELECTION OF CLOTHS FROM
THE MUSEUM OF MANKIND
THE ETHNOGRAPHY DEPARTMENT OF THE BRITISH MUSEUM
6 BURLINGTON GARDENS
LONDON W1

POSTER ART SERIES

AFRICAN TEXTILES
IS A VOLUME IN THE POSTER ART SERIES.
UP TO TEN PLATES MAY BE REPRODUCED
IN ANY ONE PROJECT OR PUBLICATION,
WITHOUT SPECIAL PERMISSION AND FREE OF CHARGE.
WHEREVER POSSIBLE THE AUTHOR, TITLE AND PUBLISHER
SHOULD BE ACKNOWLEDGED IN A CREDIT NOTE.
FOR PERMISSION TO MAKE MORE EXTENSIVE USE OF
THE PLATES IN THIS BOOK APPLICATION MUST BE MADE
TO THE PUBLISHER.

ISBN 0-517-688077

PRINTED IN ITALY

h g f e d c b a

INTRODUCTION

In addition to clothing, textiles in Africa may be used among other things as grave cloths, wall hangings, masquerade costumes, bed covers, tent awnings and, historically, as armour and currency. A large collection of fine cloth, though not a medium of exchange, may nonetheless be seen as an indication of the owner's wealth and social standing. In view of the value of cloth in African societies, it is ironic that until quite recently a figuratively carved heddle pulley from an African loom might excite more interest amongst Western ethnographers, collectors and art historians than would the many glorious woven artefacts which might have been produced on the same loom. This imbalance is partly due to our Western notion of the distinction between fine arts on the one hand and 'crafts' on the other. No such distinction exists in African societies, or if there is a distinction it could be said to be the reverse of our own. For instance, amongst people such as the Yoruba of Nigeria the ostentatious display of fine textiles is undoubtedly one of the highest forms of aesthetic expression and is one reason why Yoruba weavers continue to exploit and explore new materials and designs. In many other societies certain types of textile may be an indication of rank or the membership of a particular society or age grade. A chief or high-ranking man of the Kuba people of Zaire will accumulate large quantities of the prestigious raffia 'cut-pile' cloth (Plates 12, 14). He may give away some of this cloth to other people for the funerals of their relatives, but much of it may only be displayed at his own funerary ceremony. Thus the ultimate affirmation of his status among the living is made only after his death.

HISTORICAL BACKGROUND

The main areas of handloom weaving are today concentrated in West Africa, certain regions of North Africa, the Zaire basin and on the island of Madagascar. In addition, the making of cloth from the bark of a particular type of fig tree is still practised in Uganda (Plate 36) and Zaire, and there is evidence that barkcloth was once much more widely produced throughout the continent.

The earliest known fragments of cloth came from sites at Igbo Ukwu in Nigeria dating back to the ninth century AD, from Benin City also in Nigeria dating to the thirteenth century, and from the Tellem caves in Mali dating to the twelfth century. Early accounts by Arab travellers and, after the sixteenth century, by Europeans on the West African coast, frequently mention narrow strips of cloth, particularly as a medium of trade. These strips are the distinctive product of the double-heddle loom which is still widely used in West Africa.

LOOMS

The classification of African looms into either single- or double-heddle varieties, as suggested by Picton and Mack (*African Textiles*. London, British Museum Publications, rev. edn. 1989), is a useful descriptive distinction, the heddle being the device used to separate groups of warp threads to allow the passage of the weft. The single-heddle loom is widely distributed throughout the weaving areas of Africa, though it is mounted in a variety of positions. The vertical loom is used by the Berbers and related peoples of North Africa and in some parts of Nigeria and the Cameroon. The horizontal or ground loom is also found in these regions and, additionally, in parts of East Africa, the Sudan and Madagascar. Diagonal positioning of the single-heddle loom is found in Angola and Zaire, where it is used to weave fibres stripped from the young leaves of the raffia palm.

The double-heddle loom is found in Madagascar and Ethiopia, but is mainly associated with West Africa, where it is used to weave long strips of cloth. These may vary in width between the narrow (5 cm.) band favoured by, for instance, the Hausa (Plates 10, 11) and Nupe of Northern Nigeria, and the wider (20–30 cm.) strips commonly woven by the Mende of Sierra Leone. There are occasional variations at both ends of this scale, but the vast majority of narrow strip weave is between 10 and 15 cm. wide.

Usually the seated weaver uses pedals to operate the heddles, which are suspended above the loom. The long, horizontal warp threads are attached to a weighted sledge which is gradually drawn towards the weaver as he works. In weaving towns such as Ilorin in Nigeria it is a common sight to see as many as a dozen weavers at work, each slowly drawing his drag-weight towards him across the communal compound.

Why weave narrow strips? Nobody really knows, though there are a number of possible explanations. Wheels of narrow strip cloth made good items of trade because customers could sew together as many strips as they desired to suit their particular needs. Strips were also easily transportable, and it was far easier to maintain the quality of the cloth in this form than in large pieces which would need to be folded. There are many types of African cloth which depend for their overall pattern on the subtle juxtaposition of decorative elements on a number of individual strips placed side by side, particularly those with numerous supplementary weft float decorations and alternate warp and weft faced blocks such as the famous silk *kente* cloths of the Asante of Ghana (Plate 21).

Almost all narrow strip weaving on the double-heddle loom is done by men, whereas women weave broader pieces of cloth on a single-heddle loom except in Zaire and Angola where men weave a raffia cloth which is then intricately embroidered by women. In most cases men's narrow strip weaving is practised commercially, whereas women's weaving is usually done to fulfil domestic functions. Various sexual taboos have ensured that this division of labour has remained virtually unchanged for centuries, though there are exceptions to all these rules.

MATERIALS

Locally produced fibres which are spun into yarn include cotton, silk, wool and goatshair. Woven cloth is also produced from non-spun natural fibres such as raffia, described above, and bast which is obtained from the stems of certain plants. Locally produced African silk yarn lacks lustre and is woven into a beige coloured cloth which was nonetheless highly prized by peoples such as the Yoruba among whom it was known as *sanyan*. Among the Malagasy people silk was the preferred material for burial shrouds.

The yarn produced from hand-spun local materials is thick and hard to work with, so that in those parts of Africa which had contact with Europe before the period of colonial expansion there has been a long tradition of using imported silk and cotton yarn, of unravelling European cloths and, in more recent years, of using supplementary and in some cases subtractive techniques to embellish factory-woven cloth. Since the turn of the century synthetic yarns such as rayon have gradually replaced imported silk, and in the last twenty or thirty years lurex has become all the rage in West Africa, particularly in Nigeria (Plate 9). In addition to the new yarns which have become available, a range of imported synthetic dyes have augmented the colours already obtained from natural dyes such as black or brown from river mud, red from camwood, yellow from brimstone bark and, most important of all, indigo blue from the genus Indigofera known locally as tinto in West Africa.

DYEING

Although many cloths are woven from uncoloured natural fibres, the practice of dyeing both the yarn and the completed textile is widespread throughout Africa. In northern Nigeria the Hausa people dye factory-made cotton shirting and damask, overloading the cloth with indigo and then beating it with wooden mallets until it has acquired a wonderful irridescent sheen.

The technique known as ikat, in which warp elements are tied in groups and dyed before weaving, was practised in Western Madagascar (Plate 37) where the influence of Asian weaving traditions is a likely source; but it also occurs in West Africa, though usually in a subsidiary role of decorating perhaps a few warp stripes in a large cloth.

By far the most common method of imparting a pattern to ready woven cloth is that of rendering certain parts of the surface impervious to dye by means of various resisting agents. This is achieved through variants of two basic techniques. One method is to use raffia fibre thread to stitch folds and pleats, or to sew sticks, stones and leaves onto the cloth before dyeing. The second method is to apply starch paste to the surface, either freehand or by forcing it through a stencil.

Resist dyeing is practised widely in Nigeria where the best known exponents are the Yoruba people, but it is also found in a number of other West African countries and in Zaire. Indigo dye on white cotton shirting is the most frequent combination employed, though various other synthetic colours are used, as in the *gara* cloth of Sierra Leone, while patterned factory-made cloth and imported damask are often used as the base cloth in Togo and Senegal respectively.

The term *adire* is sometimes used to describe indigo resist dyed cloth in general, but in fact it is the name given by the Yoruba to the cloths which they produce using this technique. Almost all *adire* cloths are roughly square in shape, being composed of two rectangular pieces of cotton shirting sewn together, and they can be subdivided into two groups distinguished by the different techniques used to produce them: *adire eleko* (Plates 5, 6) in which starch is the resisting agent, and *adire oniko* (Plate 7) in which the resist is supplied by raffia fibre stitching, either on its own or in combination with other objects. Starch resist *adire*, whether handpainted or stencilled, can always be distinguished from a stitch-dyed cloth because the design only appears on one side.

As in the case of weaving, the dyeing of cloth tends to be the work of either one sex or the other, though which it is varies from society to society. For instance, among the Hausa of northern Nigeria dyeing is exclusively performed by men, whereas further south among the Yoruba people it is solely the work of women.

There are various types of dyed cloth which are not produced by either the starch or stitch methods, notably the *bogolanfini* or 'mud cloths' of the Bamana people of Mali (Plate 27). The technique is time-consuming and complex, involving several distinct stages and variations. The designs are produced on yellow-dyed cloth by filling in the areas surrounding them with black mud dye. The yellow dye is then discharged from the designs by painting over them with a caustic solution. In the finished product the designs most commonly appear white on a blackish brown background, though this colour combination may occasionally be altered by the use of different dyes.

PATCHWORK, APPLIQUÉ AND EMBROIDERY

Patchwork and appliqué are techniques quite commonly used in the production of handmade textiles, notably in the magnificent banners produced by the Fon people of the Republic of Benin and in the intricately patterned dance skirts of the Kuba people of Zaire (Plate 13). Conventional embroidery is far more widespread than patchwork or appliqué, being practised almost everywhere in Africa where cloth is produced, though it has been brought to a fine art by the Hausa people of Nigeria (Plates 10, 11) and by certain peoples of the Cameroon (Plate 32).

An interesting variant on conventional embroidery is the so called 'cut-pile' technique still practised in Zaire by the Kuba people (Plates 12, 14). A plain weave of raffia cloth is woven by men on the diagonal, single-heddle loom. Women then use a needle to draw fine threads of softened raffia fibre under individual warps and out again, as in conventional embroidery. They then pull the thread through until only a few millimetres of the end protrudes, and using a special knife, cut through the thread the same distance above the surface. The tightness of the weave is sufficient to hold the resulting U-shaped piece of fibre in place. This process is repeated thousands of times, creating a soft, velvety pile, areas of which are often combined with lines of conventional embroidery to produce some of the most beautiful and complex patterns to be seen anywhere among the textiles of Africa. Two distinct regional styles can be distinguished in Kuba cut-pile cloth: that of the Shobwa (Plate 14) who make cloths dominated by yellow and black tones with most of the surface covered in pile, and that of the Ngongo (Plate 12) in which the plain weave cloth is often dyed purple and the designs are much more widely spaced.

THE SIGNIFICANCE OF PATTERN AND COLOUR

Pattern and motifs can also, of course, be created as part of the weaving process. In addition to stripes and checks which are produced simply by grouping different coloured strands of the warp and by crossing them where desired with contrasting colours in the weft, further motifs and patterns can be created by supplementary weft floats and inlays, which are achieved by the use of extra heddles, pattern sticks and various other technical additions to the loom. Some cloths of the Asante people of Ghana were so complex in structure that six heddles were needed to weave them. Four heddles are still habitually used today.

It is over-indulgent to play 'hunt the symbol' and to attribute a significance beyond the purely decorative or descriptive to all the patterns and motifs which appear on African textiles. However, it is true that on many African cloths both the overall design and the individual patterns and motifs within it are given names which might simply be descriptive of, say, something from the natural environment or an historical event, but also might have some proverbial or aphoristic meaning. It would be wrong to conclude that a certain combination of these named patterns and motifs necessarily implies a particular ritual or ceremonial use for the cloth, but that is not to deny that these elements will not have a particular significance for the owner. For example, among Islamic peoples such as the Berber of North Africa and the Hausa of northern Nigeria, stylized designs representing implements such as knives, weaving combs or mirrors may be seen as symbolic protection against evil, having the ability to pierce the 'evil eye' or reflect the envious glance (Plates 10, 33, 34). Among the Peul of Mali the complex motif known as *landal* represents a microcosm of the natural environment inhabited by these transhumant people.

Our western perception of textile design has been coloured by the expectation of seeing an identical pattern or motif repeated within a certain area of cloth. It therefore comes as a surprise to find that African artists show an extraordinary uniformity in their taste for varying the geometric with the unexpected, the repetitive with the exceptional; and nowhere is this better exemplified than in the patterning of cloth. The inclusion of apparently deliberate 'errors' in an otherwise geometric design has fuelled speculation that they may represent a codified system of meaning, as has been suggested for the *bogolanfini* or 'mudcloths' of the Bamana people of Mali. In Islamicized areas of Africa it might reasonably be suggested that the profanity implicit in producing a geometrically perfect design has radically affected the patterning of textiles. No such claim could be made for the Kuba people of Zaire, whose culture has not been influenced by either Islam or Christendom. It has been mathematically proved that, within the rigid framework of the plain-weave raffia cloths which they embroider, Kuba women have exploited at least two-thirds of the possible ways in which a design can be repetitively varied on a surface. Patterns are named, not according to their overall design, but by particular motifs or the juxtaposition of shapes within them. Thus a wide variety of designs may be described by one pattern name. The importance to the Kuba of patterns and the naming of them can be summed up in an anecdote relating to one of the *nyimi* or kings of the Kuba who, when presented with a motor cycle by a missionary in the 1920s, was unimpressed by the machine itself, but fascinated by the marks which its tyres left in the sand. The pattern has since taken its place in the lexicon of Kuba design under the name of the king who first noticed it.

Colour also has a considerable symbolic significance in many African textiles. In Madagascar the colour red is associated with secular authority but also with mystical or metaphysical power. Interestingly enough, red has become so synonymous with these qualities that some of the burial cloths known as *lamba mena* (Plate 38) (literally 'red cloth') may not even include the colour red in their designs. Simply to call them 'red' is sufficient to suggest their power and significance.

CONCLUSION

There have been many gloomy predictions of the probable demise of handmade African cloth in the face of machine-weaving and roller-printing technology, the wholesale importation of foreign cloths, and the gradual disintegration of the political and religious structures of pre-industrial societies caused by 'Western-ization'. While it is undoubtedly true that some traditions of weaving and otherwise decorating cloth may find a dwindling market, others have been stimulated and in some cases perhaps even liberated by the changes taking place, as witnessed by the expanding production of the female weavers of Akwete in south-eastern Nigeria (Plates 1, 2, 3, 4). Although handspun yarn may be pleasing to the Western eye and touch, it is far more difficult to weave than machine-spun yarn, and the wide availability of the latter has allowed the handloom weaver to produce far greater quantities of cloth and to create patterns which would be impossible to achieve with thick, handspun yarn.

It should also be remembered that without a cheap and readily available supply of factory-made cotton shirting, a tradition such as Yoruba *adire* cloth could not have flourished in the way it has, and that unless the Asante peole had a ready supply of European silk and later rayon, the electric colours of *kente* cloth might never have delighted the eye. In a society such as that of the Yoruba which embraces change almost as a way of life, it should not be seen as a retrograde step that their textiles now sparkle with every shade of lurex.

As to the threat from imported cloth, the situation today is not so very different from the sixteenth century, when European traders' inventories show that large quantities of cloth were bartered on the Guinea coast. Africans have always acquired Asian or European cloths whenever they have had an opportunity to do so, often keeping them intact as prestige items, but sometimes unravelling them to be woven again in indigenous styles, sometimes imposing new designs upon them by dyeing or using other supplementary techniques, sometimes adapting their motifs and patterns for inclusion on locally made cloth, occasionally even altering their structure by cutting and pulling out threads to form new designs as practised by Kalabari women of southern Nigeria on imported cotton, gingham and madras cloth.

There is a tendency today to view the Western artistic and technological heritage in the context of a historical setting which never actually existed. We are in danger of applying the same notion to African art, and of considering the use of modern materials and technology as 'non-traditional' and therefore to be despised. Despite what some people would have us believe, a tradition is not necessarily something which is dead or dying; it may also be progressing and developing. In the case of African hand-made cloth, the tradition has shown remarkable versatility and the ability to adapt to change, and it is not about to expire in the immediate future.

CHRISTOPHER SPRING
CURATOR, AFRICAN COLLECTION, MUSEUM OF MANKIND
THE ETHNOGRAPHY DEPT. OF THE BRITISH MUSEUM, LONDON
FEBRUARY 1989

PLATE 1

Cloth woven from machine-spun cotton on an upright, single-heddle loom in Akwete, a village in southern Iboland, south-eastern Nigeria. Akwete weaving is produced exclusively by women and was traditionally traded to patrons in the Rivers district further to the south. This particular design is known as ikaki, *a Rivers term for the tortoise. The predominant diamond-shaped motif with projecting three-pronged 'legs' on either side may be seen as a stylized representation of this animal, which was considered to be wise and cunning and was associated with kingship and chieftaincy. Other motifs on the cloth may be zoomorphic, some possibly representing winged creatures, though it has also been suggested that they are anthropomorphic. (By courtesy of the trustees of the British Museum)*

PLATE 2

A cotton cloth with numerous supplementary weft float motifs woven from machine-spun cotton on an upright, single-heddle loom in Akwete, south-eastern Nigeria. The overall pattern of the cloth may have been inspired by woollen, machine-printed, imported English cloths which are much favoured by the traditional patrons of Akwete weaving in the Rivers area further to the south. Although the motifs on this cloth may be non-representational, their even distribution across the face of the cloth echoes the repeated, representational motifs to be found on the imported English cloth. (By courtesy of the trustees of the British Museum)

PLATE 3

Cotton cloth woven from machine-spun cotton on an upright, single-heddle loom in Akwete in south-eastern Nigeria. The supplementary weft float patterns of traditional Akwete cloth are now widely copied by women weavers from other areas of Nigeria. However, it is probable that Akwete weavers themselves learned many of their designs and techniques from Yoruba weavers of the town of Ijebu, where similar cloths were woven in three sections before being sewn together. (By courtesy of the trustees of the British Museum)

PLATE 4

A cloth woven from machine-spun cotton on an upright single-heddle loom in the village of Akwete, south-eastern Nigeria. Akwete cloths have a wider warp (sometimes over four feet) than any other cloths woven in Nigeria on the upright, single-heddle loom. A characteristic feature of Akwete cloths is that one end is wider than the other. It is a matter of debate whether this widened warp is an intentional feature or simply a natural result of the Akwete technique of weaving. (By courtesy of the trustees of the British Museum)

PLATE 5

A Yoruba resist-dyed adire *cloth made in Abeokuta town, Nigeria. The designs are applied to plain cotton sheeting by means of a metal stencil through which starch is forced. The cloth is then dyed in indigo, the starch resisting the dye. The words* ogun pari *mean in Yoruba 'war has finished' and presumably refer to the end of the Nigerian civil war. Although the official cease-fire was in January 1970, the date 4.10.70 may commemorate the announcement by General Gowon of the nine tasks to be achieved before handing over to a civilian government. The image of the king derives from an earlier cloth commemorating the installation of the new Alake of Abeokuta in the 1960s. (By courtesy of the trustees of the British Museum)*

PLATE 6

A resist-dyed adire *cloth of the Yoruba people, Nigeria. The cloth has been painted freehand with starch before dyeing in indigo. Like all* adire *cloths, it is prepared in two identical halves which are then sewn together. The name of the design is* olokun, *literally 'goddess of the sea', but by association has come to mean 'life is sweet' (wealth comes from overseas, wealth makes life sweet). (By courtesy of the trustees of the British Museum)*

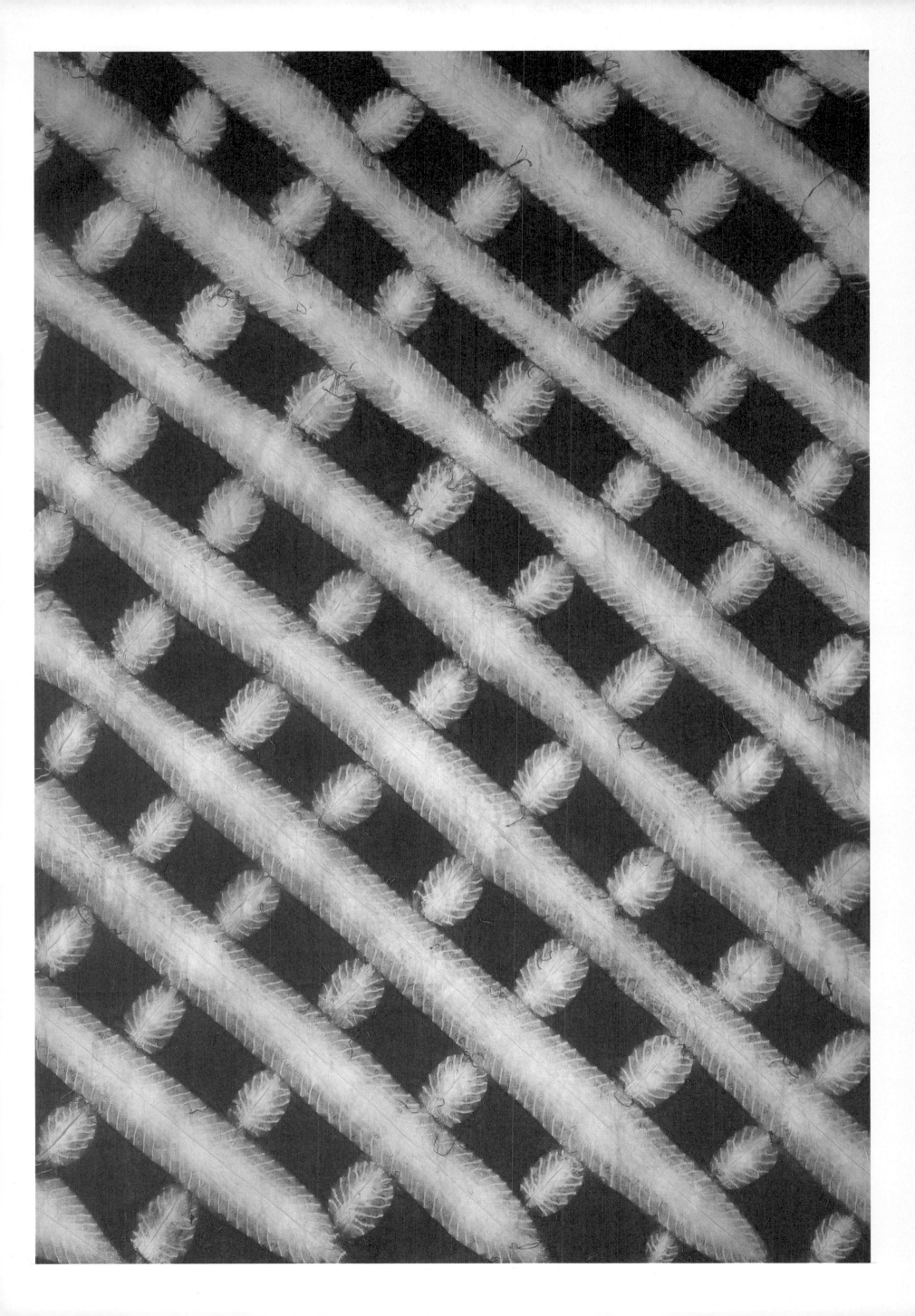

PLATE 7

Resist-dyed adire *cloth of the Yoruba people of Nigeria. The pattern is made by rolling the cloth, then stitching with raffia thread around the folds before dyeing in indigo. The remains of the raffia stitches are still visible on the cloth. The design is known as* oni koko, *'the one with cocoa', and gets its name from the similarity of the small oval motifs to cocoa pods. (By courtesy of the trustees of the British Museum)*

PLATE 8

Cloth woven of machine-spun cotton in strips 10 cm. wide with supplementary weft patterns in silk. It is typical of the type of cloth produced in the weaving centre of Ilorin, a town in northern Yorubaland, Nigeria. The cloth was probably woven in the early 1900s. (By courtesy of the trustees of the British Museum)

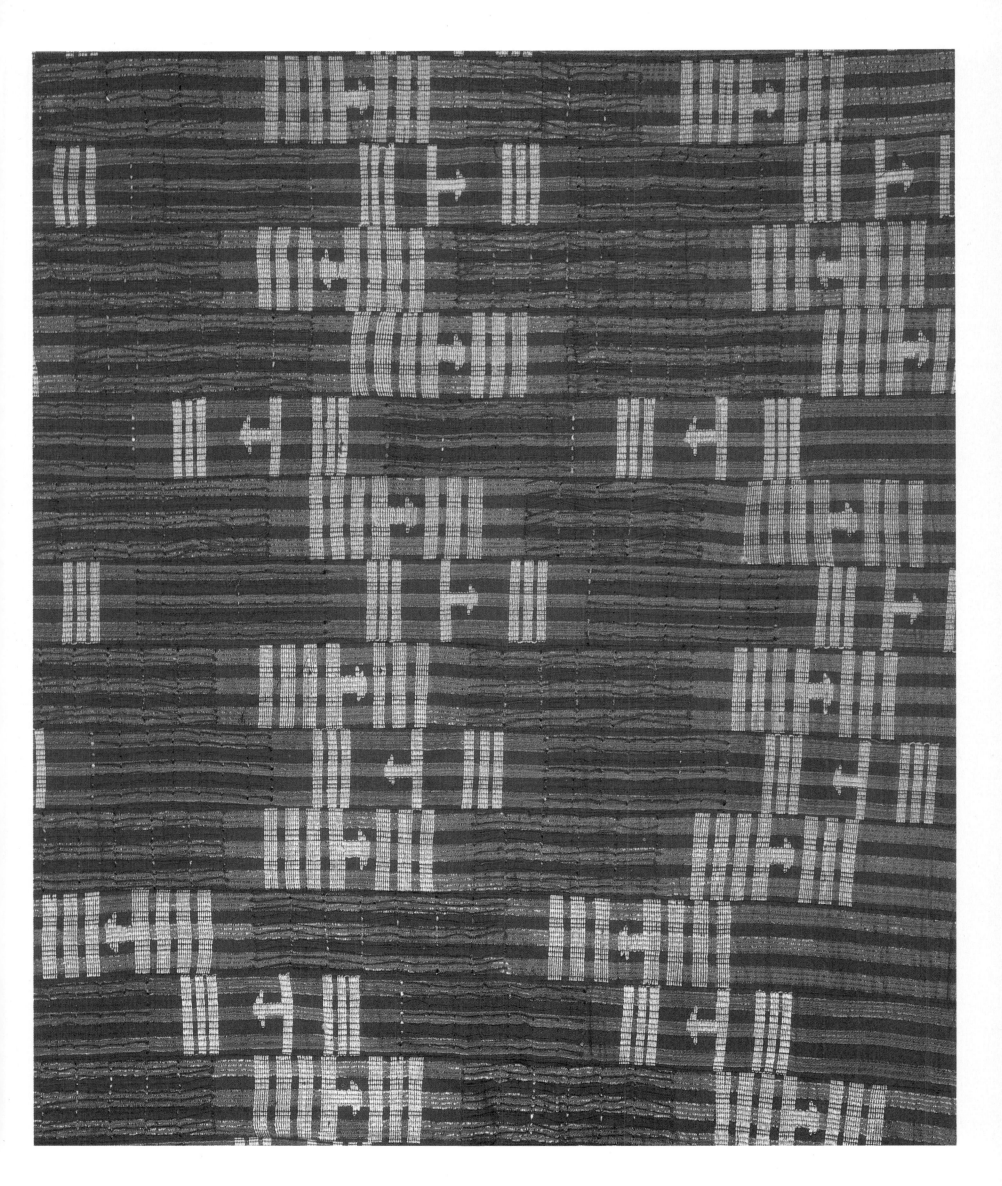

PLATE 9

A modern cloth of the Yoruba people, Nigeria. It is woven in narrow strips of magenta-dyed, machine-spun cotton, with warp stripes of green cotton and gold lurex. Each strip has sections of openwork, the holes being linked by decorative, carry-over threads. There are numerous weft inlays of yellow rayon in the form of stylized Koran boards. (By courtesy of the trustees of the British Museum)

PLATE 10

The pocket section of a man's gown of the Hausa people of northern Nigeria. The design is first painted on the narrow strip cotton cloth by a specialist other than the embroiderer. This work can be done in a few hours, though the embroidery, in European knitting wool, can take several weeks to complete. The overall pattern is known as aska takwas *('eight knives') after the eight triangular-shaped motifs, though all the other elements are also individually named. The openwork in the pattern, achieved by eyelet infilling, is picturesquely described as 'a thousand ant holes'. (By courtesy of the trustees of the British Museum)*

PLATE 11

Detail of the embroidered area on a pair of wide-waisted, draw-string trousers of the type worn by men of the Hausa people, northern Nigeria. The embroidery is executed by men in European knitting wool on narrow strip cotton cloth, and is quite distinct from the monochrome embroidery of a man's gown (Plate 10). Curiously enough, the trousers would rarely be seen as they would be covered by the gown unless the wearer was on horseback. The Islamic 'knot' motif is repeated several times in the pattern. (By courtesy of the trustees of the British Museum)

PLATE 12

Two raffia cloths produced by the Ngongo sub-group of the Kuba people of Zaire. The ground weave for the cloth is produced by male weavers on the diagonal, single-heddle loom, using fibres from the young leaves of the raffia palm. Women then decorate the cloth with additional raffia, sometimes using conventional embroidery, sometimes employing the 'cut-pile' technique in which individual pile threads are cut off close to the surface to create a texture which has been likened to velvet. In these examples the ground weave was dyed purple before the cloth was embroidered. The fibres used for the darker areas of the design were dyed before 'cut-pile' embroidery. Plain raffia has been used for the lighter areas. (By courtesy of the trustees of the British Museum)

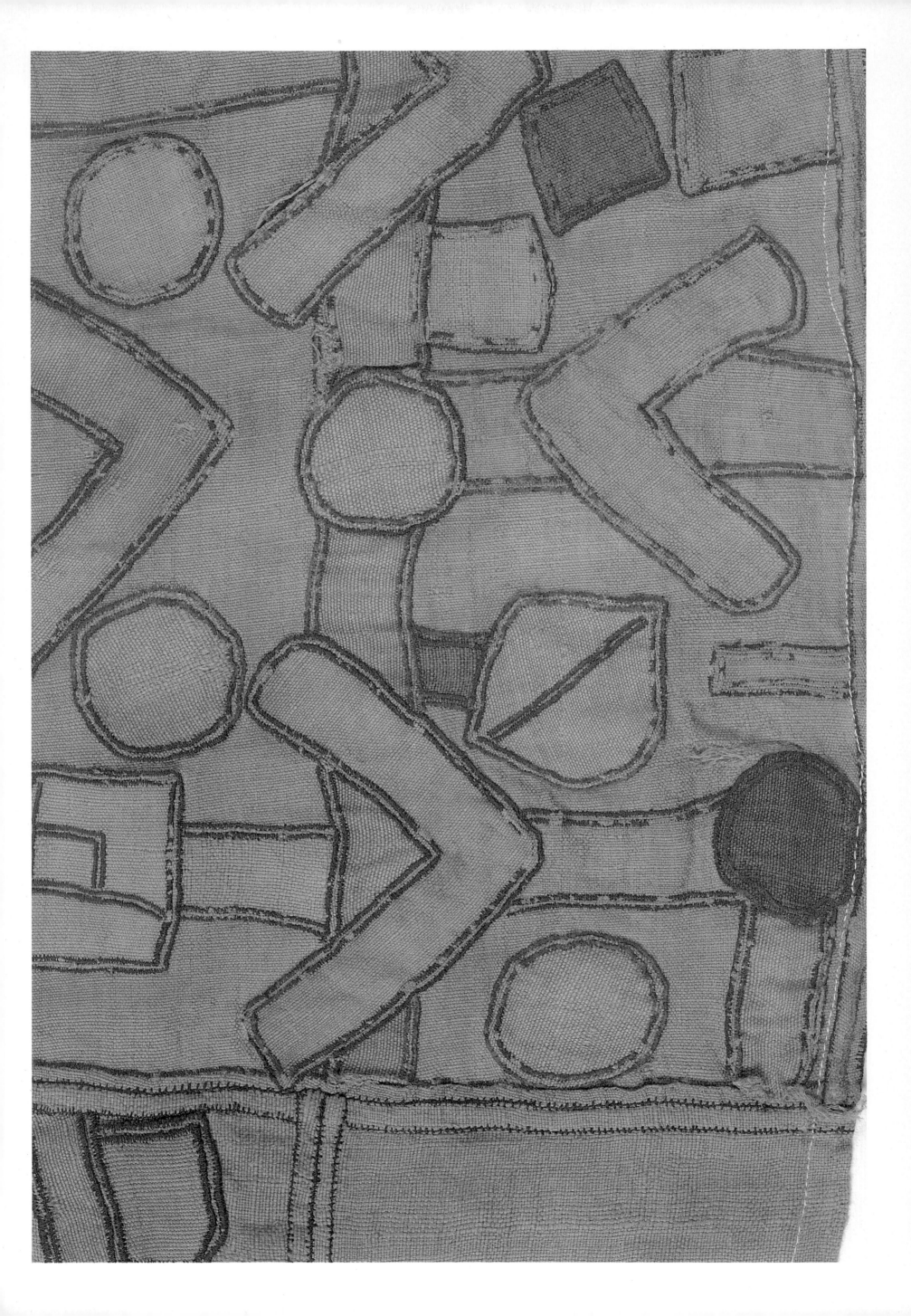

PLATE 13

Raffia dance skirt of the Kuba people of Zaire, decorated with appliqué motifs. The predominant comma-shaped motif called shinna mboa ('the tail of a dog') seems to be derived from the patch traditionally used to repair tears in plain raffia cloths. The Kuba then realized the design potential of this shape and began to use it as a decorative motif. Older cloths have just a few patches, but in more recent examples such as this the pattern has grown and multiplied into a mass of interlinked motifs. (By courtesy of the trustees of the British Museum)

PLATE 14

Raffia 'cut-pile' cloth produced by the Shobwa sub-group of the Kuba people of Zaire. Yellow and black are usually the predominant colours in Shobwa cloths, and the surface of the cloth is almost completely covered by large areas of soft, velvety 'cut-pile' and lines of conventional embroidery. In this example irregularities both of pattern and of colour have been deliberately introduced to vary the overall design. (By courtesy of the trustees of the British Museum)

PLATE 15

A 'cut-pile' raffia cloth of the Pende people of Zaire, woven in the late nineteenth century. The whole cloth, with the exception of the tips of the fringes, has been coloured with a vegetable dye after weaving and subsequent embroidery. Today the only exponents of the craft of 'cut-pile' embroidery are the Kuba people living to the east of the Pende, though Kuba oral history maintains that they learned the technique from the Pende. However, Kuba 'cut-pile' cloth never employs the identical, repeated motifs and the regular geometric shapes which are a feature of this Pende cloth. (By courtesy of the trustees of the British Museum)

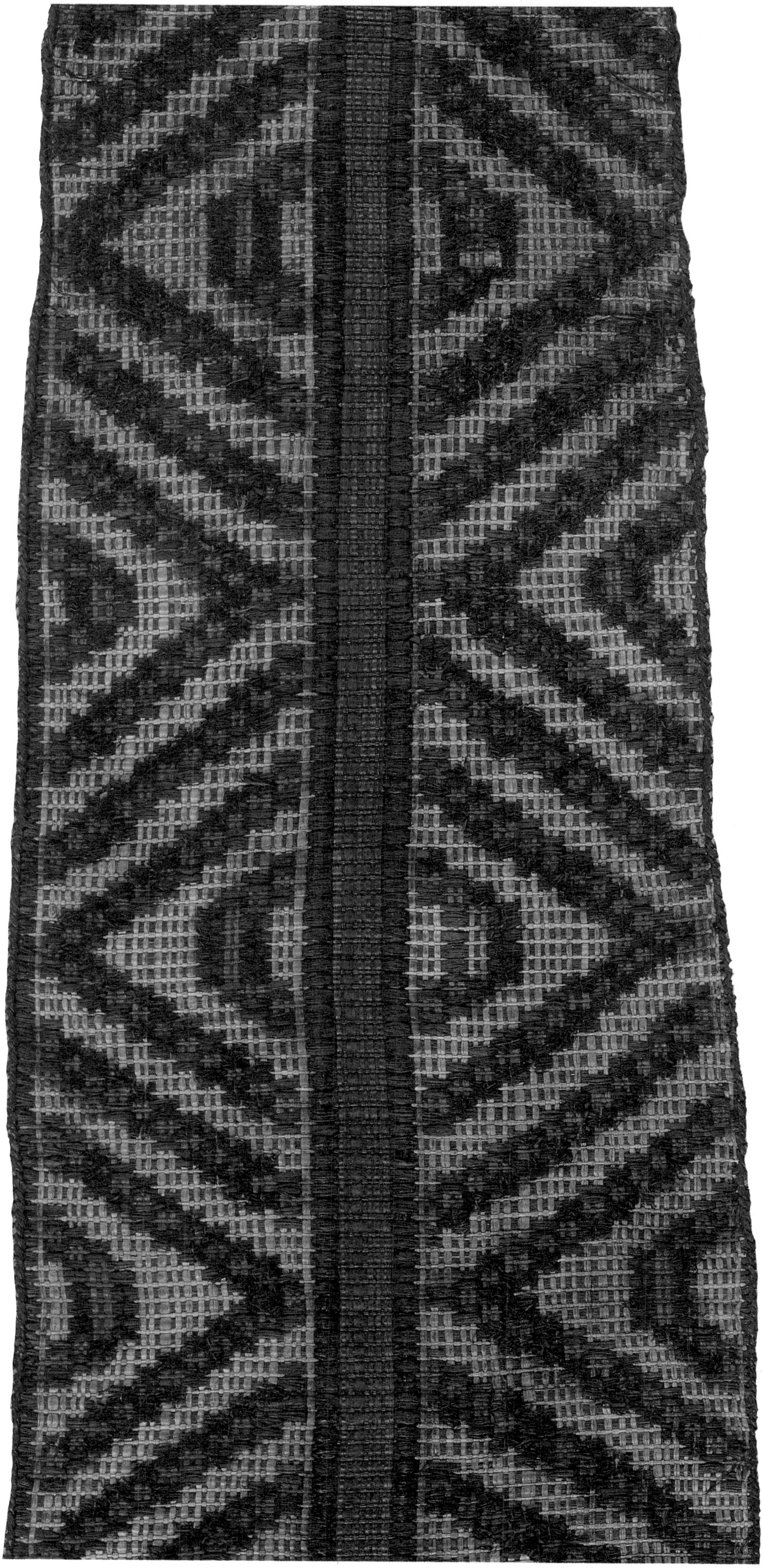

PLATE 16

A raffia mat woven by the Akela people of Zaire in the late nineteenth or early twentieth century. The Akela loom is furnished with numerous additional heddles to permit the weaving of complex, geometric patterns. This mat was collected on the behalf of the British Museum by Emil Torday, a Hungarian born ethnographer who made two expeditions to Zaire in the early years of the twentieth century. Although raffia cloths had long been traded down to the coast at the mouth of the Zaire river, little was known about the cultures which had produced them until Torday's expeditions. (By courtesy of the trustees of the British Museum)

PLATE 17

A chequerboard cloth of the Mende people, Sierra Leone, woven of hand-spun cotton in weft-faced strips 15 cm. wide, with occasional supplementary inlay motifs. This particular design is known as ki gbembele, *meaning simply 'chequerboard', but the cloth belongs to a larger group of weft-dominated designs known collectively as* kpokpo. *(By courtesy of the trustees of the British Museum)*

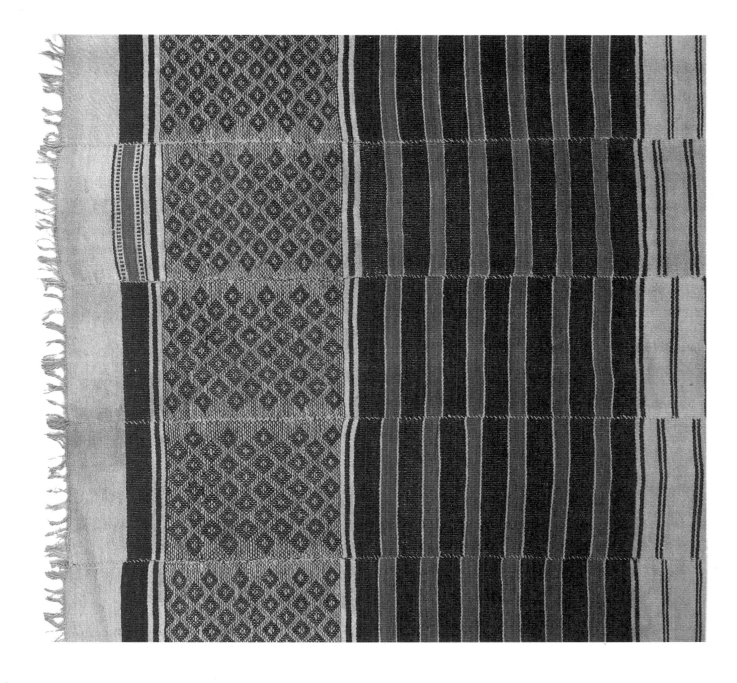

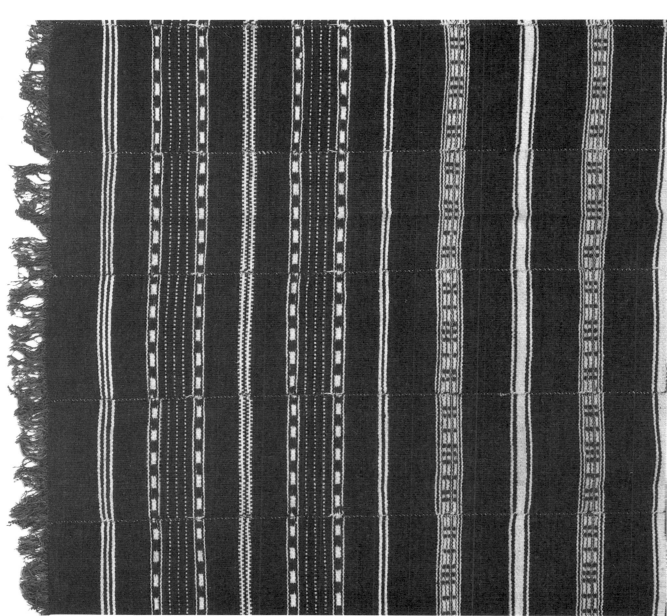

PLATE 18a

A weft-faced kpokpo *woven in strips 16 cm. wide by the Vai people of Sierra Leone. Unlike warp-faced cloths which are used for various domestic functions, weft-dominated cloths of this type are intended to demonstrate the wealth and prestige of their owners. They are often used as wall hangings or to cover a dais at funerals or state ceremonies. (By courtesy of the trustees of the British Museum)*

PLATE 18b

A weft-banded cotton cloth probably woven by Mandingo weavers of Guinea and traded into Sierra Leone. The cloth has stylistic similarities with the type of weaving still practised in Guinea Bissau which originated among weavers from the Cape Verde islands who are thought to have learned their complex designs from the Portuguese in the sixteenth century (see Plate 19). (By courtesy of the trustees of the British Museum)

PLATE 19

A cotton cloth from Guinea Bissau woven of machine-spun yarn in strips about 18 cm. wide. The complex supplementary weft patterns in blue and black are woven with the aid of several dozen string heddles. Among the few examples of European influence on the design of African textiles, the patterns are thought to have been introduced by the Portuguese to the weavers from West Africa whom they took as slaves to the Cape Verde islands during the sixteenth century. This style of weaving is still practised by the Manjako and Pepel peoples of Guinea Bissau, though now defunct on the Cape Verde islands themselves. (By courtesy of the trustees of the British Museum)

PLATE 20

An indigo-dyed cotton cloth woven from machine-spun yarn in five broad strips 22 cm. wide. There are numerous rayon supplementary float patterns in the weft. The cloth is thought to be from Ghana, though it displays some of the characteristics associated with Manjako weaving from Guinea Bissau. Its true origin still remains a mystery. (By courtesy of the trustees of the British Museum)

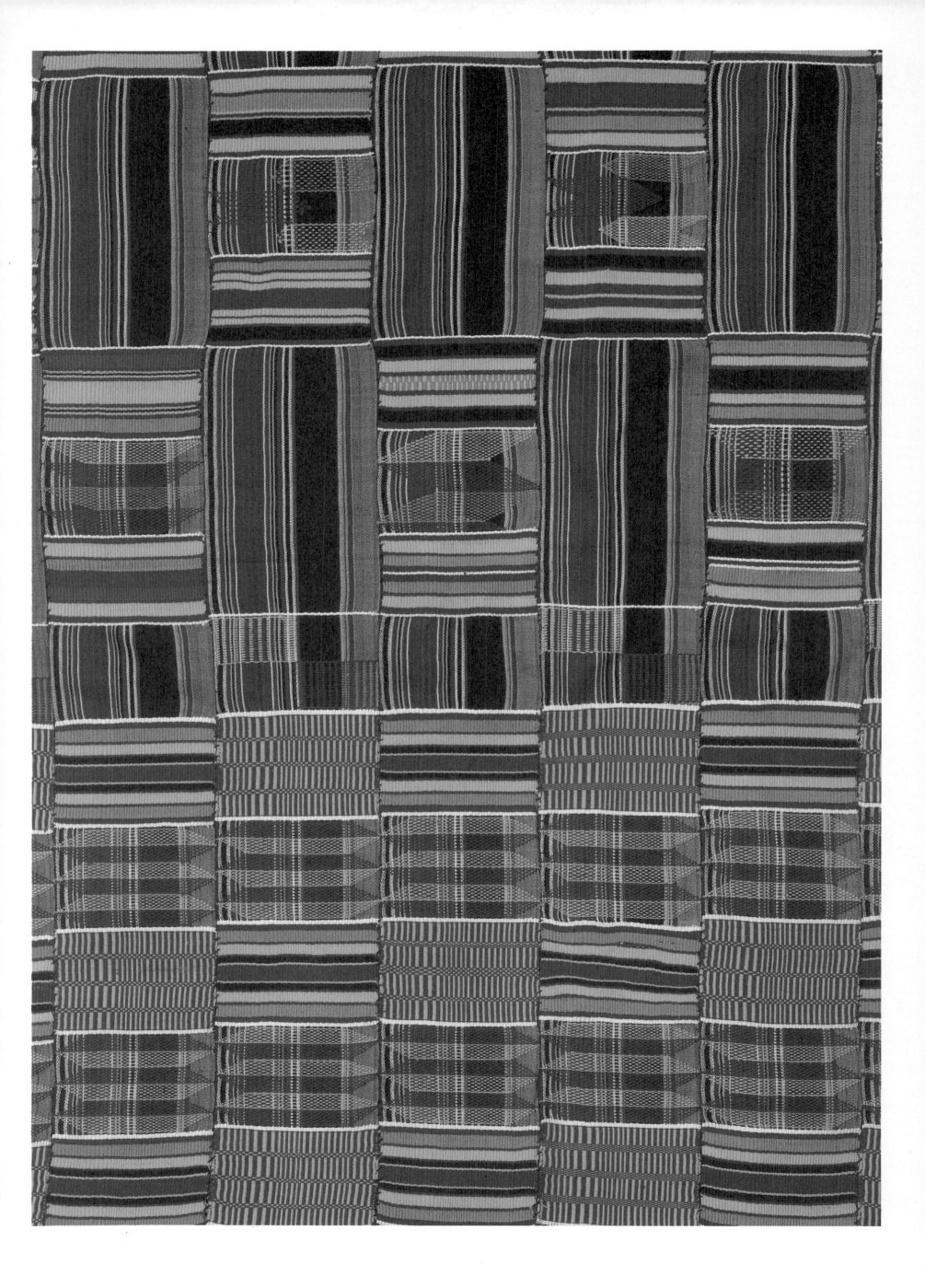

PLATE 21

An Asante silk kente *cloth from Ghana, woven in warp-faced strips 9 cm. wide, with numerous weft-faced blocks and supplementary float designs. Each strip of* kente *cloth is normally eight to ten feet long and begins and ends with a group or 'head' of five design blocks. The red and gold design consisting of alternate vertical lines and rows of dots, which may be seen on this cloth, is commonly used on the 'head' of* kente *strips and is known as* nnwotoa, *literally 'snail's bottom'. The name of the overall pattern of* kente *cloths is derived from the warp striping, though the designs incorporated in the weft are also all given names which may have a proverbial as well as purely descriptive significance. The wearing of* kente *cloth was once the prerogative of the Asantehene (king) and certain other high-ranking chiefs, but today* kente *is worn by many Ghanaians on formal occasions. (By courtesy of the trustees of the British Museum)*

PLATE 22

A modern Asante rayon cloth from Ghana, woven in plain-weave, weft-faced strips 12 cm. wide and decorated with supplementary float motifs in gold. Although this cloth has elements in common with traditional kente, *the overall pattern is not dissimilar to some cloths being woven in centres such as the town of Niamey in Niger. (By courtesy of the trustees of the British Museum)*

PLATE 23

A cotton cloth of the Ewe people, Ghana, woven in strips about 10 cm. wide. This type of textile is sometimes referred to as 'Keta' cloth because it was originally produced in the coastal town of that name, though the centre of weaving has now moved inland to Agbozume. Ewe weavers employ similar techniques to the neighbouring Asante, using a second pair of heddles on their looms to produce the supplementary float patterns. (By courtesy of the trustees of the British Museum)

PLATE 24

A warp-faced 'Keta' cloth woven from machine-spun cotton in strips about 8 cm. wide by weavers of the Ewe people of Ghana. The supplementary float patterns are reminiscent of the motifs employed by Asante weavers, though the Asante never include naturalistic motifs such as the pair of fishes on this cloth. While this example is characteristically Ewe in style, the Ewe do produce cloths which are so similar to the famous Asante kente *that it is often difficult to tell them apart. (By courtesy of the trustees of the British Museum)*

PLATE 25

Two pattern samples showing motifs employed by the Asante people of Ghana in making the hand-printed cloths known as adinkra. *The motifs are applied to cotton cloth using stamps cut from pieces of gourd. The dye used is prepared from tree bark boiled up with lumps of iron slag. The overall design of* adinkra *cloths is built up in squares of individual motifs repeated as many as thirty or forty times. As in the woven cloth of the Asante, each motif is given a name which may have a magical, historical or proverbial significance, and the overall pattern of the cloth is also named. Asante* adinkra *cloth seems to have evolved from an earlier tradition of hand-painting cloth. (By courtesy of the trustees of the British Museum)*

PLATE 26

An indigo-dyed cotton cloth of the Dogon people of Mali, composed of narrow strips 13 cm. wide and decorated with embroidery, stitchwork and eyelet open-work. This cloth is a marriage shawl worn by brides on their wedding day and for a few days afterwards. Subsequently it is worn only on feast days or at other important rituals. (By courtesy of the trustees of the British Museum)

PLATE 27

An example of the so-called 'mud cloth' or bogolanfini *of the Bamana people of Mali. The pattern is produced on a yellow-dyed, narrow-strip cotton cloth by painting with river mud to form the dark areas, and then discharging the dye from the lighter areas using a caustic solution. The recurring linear pattern at the top of the cloth is said to imitate the body of a crocodile, the double zig-zag motifs the legs of a cricket. The deliberate irregularities in the design may represent some coded system of meaning, though variations on an otherwise regular pattern are characteristic of many other types of African textile. (By courtesy of the trustees of the British Museum)*

PLATE 28

A woollen blanket, khasa, *woven from hand-spun yarn in strips 20 cm. wide by the Peul people of Mali. The motifs which appear on the blankets are all named. Most common, and in some ways most important, is the combination of diamonds and triangles known as* bitjirgal, *a maternity and fertility symbol representing the female body in stylized form. Thick blankets like this perform many functions, notably to protect their owners not only from the cold at night, but also from the mosquitoes. Appropriate enough, among the Peul all blankets and covers are collectively known as* sudumare *('the house'). (By courtesy of the trustees of the British Museum)*

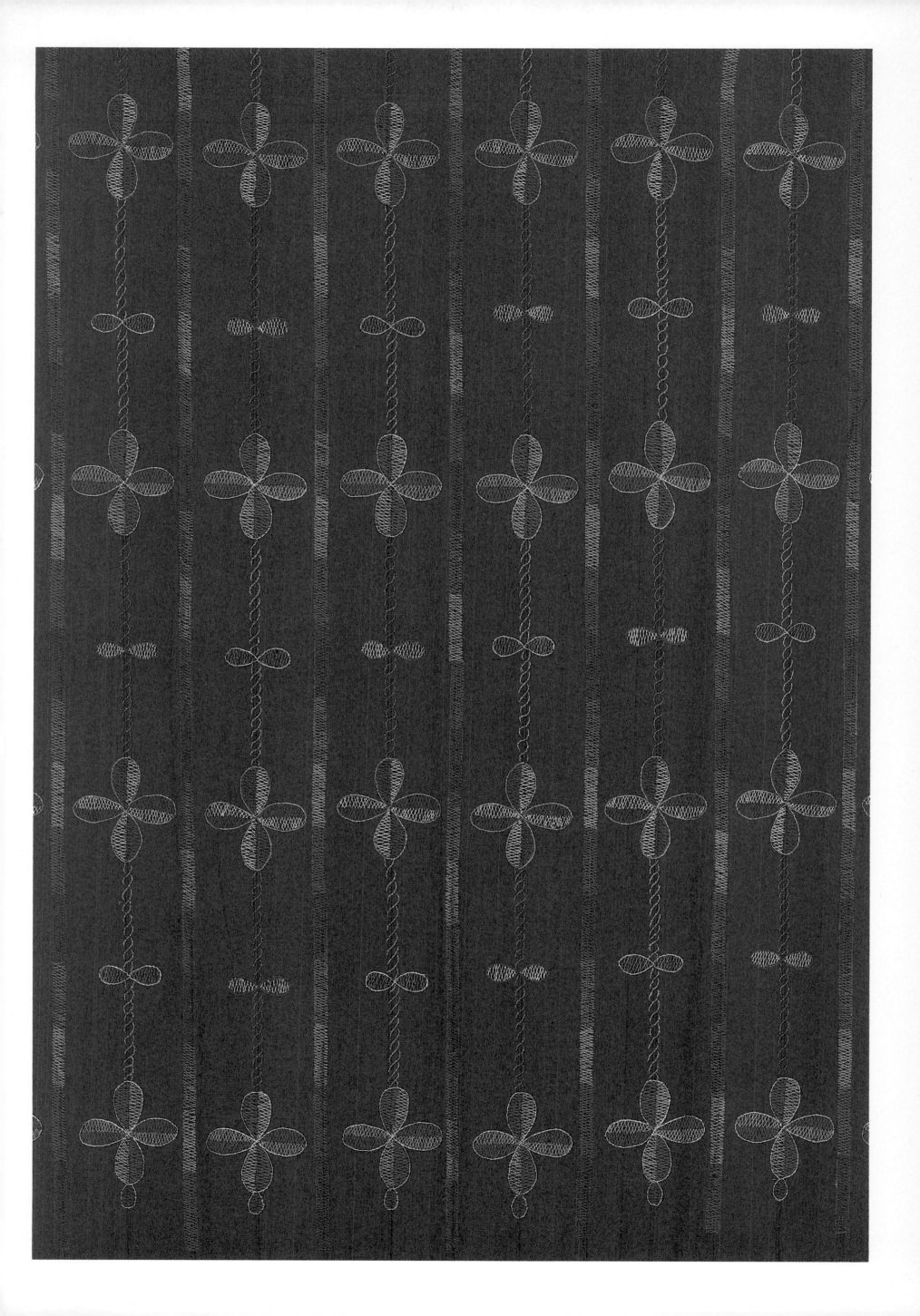

PLATE 29

An indigo-dyed cotton cloth composed of very narrow (6 cm.) woven strips, and embroidered in imported European thread using herringbone cross-stitches. The cloth may have been woven in Senegal or Gambia, but little else is known about it. (By courtesy of the trustees of the British Museum)

PLATE 30

European imported red and yellow printed fabric, stitched with raffia thread before being dyed with indigo. The cloth is thought to have been produced in Ghana or Togo. Though often applied to plain cotton sheeting, the use of the 'tie and dye' technique on an already patterned and coloured cloth produces interesting results. (By courtesy of the trustees of the British Museum)

PLATE 31

A cotton cloth thought to be from Senegal or Gambia, woven in alternate warp- and weft-faced narrow (5 cm.) strips with occasional supplementary weft inlays in different coloured yarn. An interesting detail is that the thin stripe running through the weft-faced strips is an example of the seersucker technique, rare in West African textiles, in which a group of warp threads are deliberately loosened to create a puckered rib running the length of the cloth. (By courtesy of the trustees of the British Museum)

PLATE 32

Detail of a gown from the grasslands area of Cameroon, similar to the type often worn by the Bamenda people. The garment has been embroidered with imported, synthetically dyed wool on machine-made cotton cloth. These gowns are worn on many important ceremonial occasions. The designs are probably influenced by similar decorative devices used by Jukun weavers in neighbouring Nigeria. (By courtesy of the trustees of the British Museum)

PLATE 33

A silk textile from Algeria woven in a single strip, 55 cm. wide, by male urban Arab weavers in the early 1900s, probably using a Jacquard-type mechanized drawloom. The number five, khamsa, *is a regular feature of the patterning on Islamic textiles, often rendered in the form of a hand as in this example. However, it has more than a decorative function in that it is thought to protect the owner against evil. Sharp objects such as a weaving comb or the straight fingers of the hand can pierce the evil eye. It is the fingers of the hand which are referred to in the common Arabic insult 'there's five in your eye'. (By courtesy of the trustees of the British Museum)*

PLATE 34

A Berber woollen textile from Algeria, woven in a single strip 45 cm. wide on an upright, single-heddle loom. Unlike urban weaving in Algeria, which is normally performed by Arab men, rural weaving is exclusively done by women. Once again the khamsa, *or group of five, appears, though this time in the form of five interlinked squares. (By courtesy of the trustees of the British Museum)*

PLATE 35

A camel saddle cloth from Ethiopia. The green areas are appliqué leather cut-outs sewn on with woollen thread. The floral and geometric motifs are embroidered in wool. The base cloth is of cotton. (By courtesy of the trustees of the British Museum)

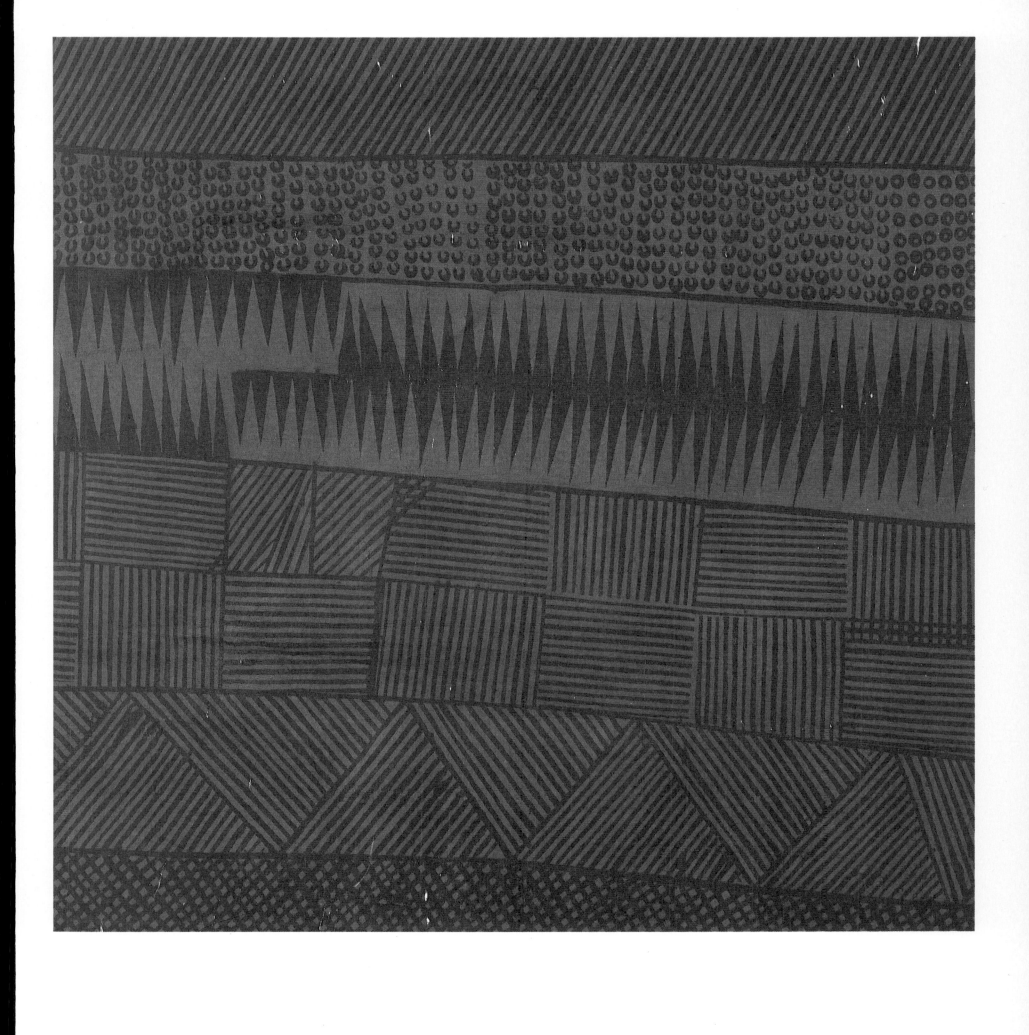

PLATE 36

Detail of a large, decorated barkcloth of the Ganda people of Uganda, probably produced in the late nineteenth century. Barkcloth in Uganda is manufactured by beating the softened bark of a particular species of fig tree until it is almost paper-thin. The designs on the cloth are non-representational and in this particular example have been both stamped and painted freehand onto the cloth. Sometimes the Ganda use a stencil cut from a banana leaf to apply designs to their barkcloth. (By courtesy of the trustees of the British Museum)

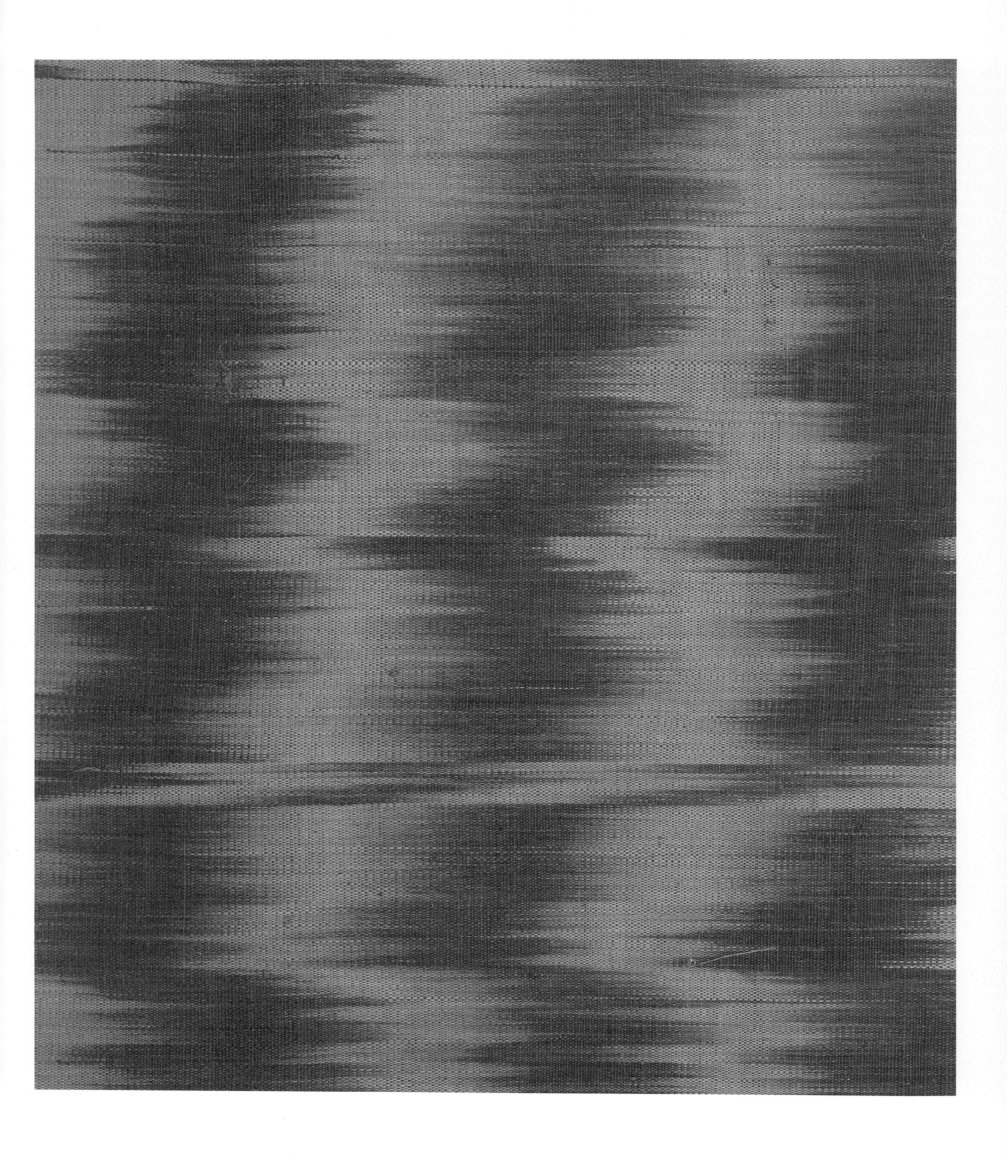

PLATE 37

Ikat-dyed raffia cloth, produced by the Sakalava people of Western Madagascar. The technique of ikat, in which groups of warps are tied together and dyed before weaving, may be clearly seen in the loose warp elements forming the fringe of this cloth. Although this is a simple example, the Malagasy weave highly complex ikat cloths, and it is a technique associated with the Asian source of much in Malagasy culture in general. (By courtesy of the trustees of the British Museum)

PLATE 38

A silk textile woven in three broad strips, each 44 cm. wide, by the Merina people of Madagascar. The pattern and colour of this textile are distinctive of styles that developed amongst the different aristocratic ranks of the nineteenth-century kingdom of Imerina. Blue/green was a colour reserved for the royal clan and this example may well be of such origin. This type of textile would have been worn as a shawl by the living but might subsequently also be put to service as a shroud. Although red is not a predominant colour in the cloth, it would have been described as a lamba mena *(literally 'red cloth'). Red is a highly significant colour to the Malagasy, denoting both secular authority and supernatural power. (By courtesy of the trustees of the British Museum)*

PLATE 39

A cotton and silk warp-faced textile, lamba, *woven in three strips each 63 cm. wide, probably by the Merina people of Madagascar. The border of the cloth is decorated with small silver beads, which are strung on the warps and then woven in with the wefts in such a way that they are visible on both sides of the cloth. (By courtesy of the trustees of the British Museum)*

PLATE 40

A cotton and plastic textile of the Merina people of Madagascar. Although not distinctively African either in the weaving technique or in the materials used, the cloth nonetheless demonstrates an ingenuity in the creative use of waste materials which is characteristically African. The ground weave is of colourless plastic fibres into which off-cuts and pieces of waste cotton have been introduced as elements in the weft. This produces a thick cloth which is used as a blanket in the colder, highland regions of Madagascar. (By courtesy of the trustees of the British Museum)